Lift Off With Rocket Stoves

Jason & Miranda Chiasson

SKIPPY'S INTRODUCTION

Skippy: "Man, I love rocket stoves. I was disappointed when I first learned they had nothin' to do with flying to the moon, but they grew on me when I learned I could use 'em to cook bacon. Now I use rocket stoves every day, and that's why I wrote this book."

Boss: "Skippy, you didn't write the book."

Skippy: "Huh? Whaddya mean I didn't write the book? Just 'cuz I can't read doesn't mean I can't write a book."

Boss: "Oh come on now Skippy, we just asked you for a couple of your favorite meals for ideas."

Skippy: "Exactly. That's what I'm sayin'. I'm the inspiration for the whole book."

Boss: "We asked the rest of the team for their favorites too, Skippy. It was a team effort."

Skippy: "Well Boss, you can spin it any way you want. But I'm gonna give the introduction to the book so everyone knows. Just you watch."

Boss: "Yeah okay Skippy, we'll see about that."

TABLE OF CONTENTS

THIS BOOK

We wrote this book to provide a practical introduction to rocket stoves. They're fun little contraptions, and our goal with this book is to help you get to the fun part as fast as possible.

That said, we know the word "fun" means something different for everyone. The first part of this book is a little background on our story, and a brief history of rocket stoves. If that's not your thing, then no worries. We made sure to organize the book so you can hop straight to the parts you want. No need to read every page!

Real quick though, just so we're all on the same page (no pun intended)...

This book is not:

- A guide on how to build rocket stoves
- A full history of rocket stoves
- A detailed comparison of different models of stoves
- An expert recipe book with exact instructions

Instead, we like to consider this a crash course on rocket stoves with a few simple recipes to get you started.

So if that sounds like it floats your boat, then welcome! We hope you enjoy reading this book as much as we enjoyed putting it together.

Have fun!

 P.S. You can also check out this book's companion website, **chiassonsmoke.com/rocket-stove-book,** where you can find tutorial videos, recommended sauces and spices, and more!

OUR STORY

Hey Y'all,

Jason and Miranda here from Chiasson Smoke. We're excited to introduce you to the world of rocket stoves and how they can make your life a bit more fun.

But what would an introduction be without a little background on where our fire got started? It's been a long journey, and believe us when we tell you we haven't always been making rocket stoves.

BEGINNINGS

Our story began on a ranch in Montana in 2007. Before that year, we had never really wondered what happens when a Wisconsin girl meets a Louisiana boy far from home. But life gave us the answer, and it turned out to be a partnership that changed our lives.

We spent several years together tending to the ranch, riding horses, and team roping, until we realized it was time to tie the permanent knot together. In 2013, we could finally call ourselves "The Chiassons", and this new life of ours was just getting started.

We moved to Jason's home state of Louisiana, where we settled down for a few years. During that time, we were blessed with our daughter Brooklyn. It would be a little while before the family tree grew more branches, but first, we had to relocate.

CHIASSON SMOKE

After six years in Louisiana, it was time for our next adventure. In 2018, we packed our bags and headed to the family farm in Wisconsin, using the metalwork experience we had accumulated over the years to start our very own welding shop: Chiasson Smoke.

It was during this time that we welcomed our son Austin into the world, and our youngest son Clay shortly after that. I guess we weren't busy enough trying to get our new business off the ground!

Family had always been our priority, and Chiasson Smoke didn't change that one bit. We would pick on each other at the shop, teach the kids how to help out, and find those little moments to appreciate the absurdity of life during hectic times running the business. But in everything we did, we did it together as a family. And soon, to our surprise, we'd have a lot more people participating.

SHARING OUR ADVENTURES

In the spring of 2020, we decided to share our daily shenanigans with the world by making some videos of our shop and uploading them to TikTok and Instagram. We didn't know what to expect at the time, but amassing hundreds of thousands followers was absolutely not something we would have imagined.

Since our first uploads, we've had the privilege of sharing our adventures with millions of people from around the world. Viewers have had a chance to witness our serious moments, silly antics, quirky sense of humor, and of course, our world-class acting skills. (...We wish!)

Our supporters watched our small family business struggle during the hard times, learn during the enlightening ones, and grow further than we had ever imagined during the lucky ones. This shared adventure has changed our lives, and we couldn't have done it without each and every one of you. We're humbled.

Whether you've been with us since the early days, or just yesterday discovered the rocket stove rabbit hole, we want to thank you wholeheartedly for your support.

It's hard to put in writing just how much this journey means to us, and we're privileged to have been able to share it with you all.

Thank you for being part of our story.

- Jason and Miranda

ROCKET STOVES

Alright, I suppose we should start with the basics: What are "rocket" stoves? Well, contrary to what our friend Skippy thinks, they have nothing to do with astronaut food.

What separates rocket stoves from traditional stoves is their efficiency. Rocket stoves burn small pieces of wood in a way that produces more heat and less smoke. They've been embraced by homesteading communities, campers, and DIY welders. They've even played a part in saving the world, helping people in developing countries cook safely where resources are scarce.

Nowadays, rocket stoves can be used by just about anyone who wants to give them a try. And that's exactly what we hope this book encourages you to do!

ORIGINS

The concepts behind rocket stoves date back to the ancient Romans, who built sophisticated air flow systems to heat buildings. These early examples laid the groundwork for efficient stoves and heaters.

Over the centuries, the concepts have been recycled time and again for different stoves and lamps. Eventually, we landed on the modern day rocket stove design.

ROCKET STOVES TODAY

The modern design for what we now call "rocket stoves" was invented by the late Dr. Larry Winiarski in the 1980s. Dr. Winiarski dedicated his career to building safe and efficient stove designs, and teaching locals in developing countries to build their own.

Thanks to the generosity of Dr. Winiarski, who made the decision to keep the design open-source rather than patenting it, we now have an abundance of designs in use today. Many people opt to build their own from scrap materials, continuing the tradition of innovation and community sharing.

Here at Chiasson Smoke, we try to strike a balance between the satisfaction of DIY building, and the elegance of modern design. That's why we offer DIY rocket stove weld kits and plans for those of us who like to get our hands dirty, and of course, fully assembled builds for the rest of us.

EFFICIENCY AND BENEFITS

Rocket stoves are renowned for their efficiency. They use small pieces of wood and produce a hot, clean burn, which means less fuel is needed and less smoke is produced. This efficiency translates to significant environmental benefits, and better bang for your buck.

Economically, rocket stoves are cost-effective, and not only offer a safe and affordable design for families in developing countries, but also offer a practical solution for anyone looking to reduce their fuel consumption and live more sustainably.

COMMUNITY AND CULTURAL IMPACT

Rocket stoves have been embraced by a wide range of communities. Homesteaders take pride in the self-sufficiency rocket stoves offer. DIY enthusiasts enjoy the satisfaction of building their own stoves. And campers value the portability and efficiency of rocket stoves for outdoor cooking.

Globally, rocket stoves have been adopted in various countries and cultures, providing a simple yet powerful tool for improving living conditions and promoting sustainable practices.

BUILDING YOUR OWN ROCKET STOVE

One of the most appealing aspects of rocket stoves is that they can be built from readily available materials, including scrap. There are lots of resources available online to guide you through the process of building your own rocket stove.

ROCKET STOVE DESIGN

If you've picked up one of the Chiasson Smoke rocket stove models, you'll want to familiarize yourself with the parts.

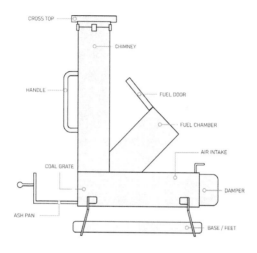

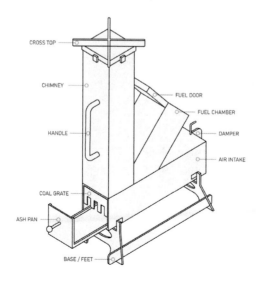

CHIMNEY	The vertical tube, which carries the fire and heat
FUEL CHAMBER	The diagonal tube where you put your wood and other fuel
FUEL DOOR	A small door on the fuel chamber
AIR INTAKE TUBE	The horizontal tube, which is responsible for letting air inside the stove
DAMPER	The rotating "door" that controls the amount of air that goes through the air intake
COAL GRATE	A grate connected to the air intake which sits just below the fuel chamber and chimney; It keeps the fuel in place while allowing ashes to fall onto the ash pan.
ASH PAN	The pan that slides in and out of the air intake tube. It sits just below the coal grate.
HANDLE	A carry handle to make life a little easier
CROSS TOP	A removable attachment that connects to the chimney and allows you to place a pan or pot on the stove
BASE / FEET	A base with feet that keeps the rocket stove stable; This is removable and collapsible in the 1612 model.

Optional parts:

GRILL TOP	The vertical tube, which carries the fire and heat
GRIDDLE TOP	Replaces the cross top with a griddle

LET'S GET STARTED

Now that you have a little background on what the heck these stoves are, it's time for the fun part- getting that stove up and running so we can cook some food!

COOKING ON YOUR ROCKET STOVE

Years ago, I had a boss that let us take hour-long lunches and grill up some food right at work. It wasn't just the extra break that I enjoyed... Grilling with the team brought us together and made the job feel like less of a chore.

To this day, I remember him as my favorite boss. And I've always told myself that, if I were ever fortunate enough to have my own business and a team helping me out, I'd do the same thing.

By some stroke of luck I still can hardly believe, we've had the privilege of growing the team, and I've been able to continue the tradition of hour-long grill sessions for lunch. Of course, we do it the Chiasson Smoke way, and usually use rocket stoves.

As you've probably guessed, we love cooking on rocket stoves, especially since they're absolutely perfect for camping and other group activities.

But you know, cooking outdoors by yourself is also a great way to calm your mind.

And at the end of the day, when that stove has cooled off, you can even use it to hold your beer! (Or fire it up again and make more hot dogs, as my son would suggest.)

So let's quickly go over the how-to, and then we'll give you a good list of easy meals to get you started!

HOW THE "PROS" DO IT

Okay, so I admit, I'm no chef. But that's one of the best parts of cooking on rocket stoves– you don't need to be a pro!

Here's all you need to get things going.

First of all, as we touched on above, there are tons of different types of rocket stoves. Most of our advice will be tailored to our own 1612 and Bulldog rocket stove models, but you should be able to take the ideas and use them on other models.

GETTING THE FIRE STARTED

Get some fuel into the fuel chamber. You can use wood logs, brush, or even twigs if that's all you have.

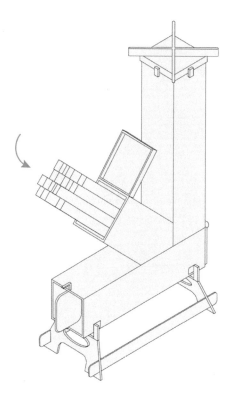

The easiest way I've found to get things started, is to just remove the ash pan, and light the fuel with a propane torch right at the coal grate on the back of the stove.

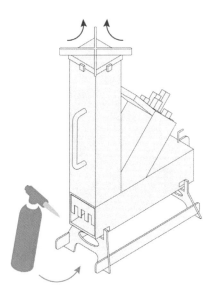

Of course, if you don't have a propane torch, you can place some fire starter right on the ash pan, light it, then slide the ash pan back in.

In either case, make sure the damper is all the way open to allow enough airflow to keep the fire going.

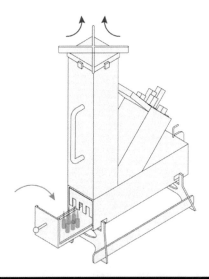

KEEPING THE FIRE GOING

Our rocket stoves are built to automatically feed the unburned fuel into the chamber, so you can pretty much just load up the fuel, light it, and let it take care of itself.

However, as ash begins to build up inside the stove, you'll notice that airflow becomes more restricted and the fire doesn't burn as well.

All you need to do in that situation, is remove your ash pan and dispose of the ashes, then put the ash pan right back in. No need to stop what you're doing. (Another good reason to call them "rocket" stoves!)

Occasionally, you'll need to add more fuel, so just keep an eye out on what you got left inside the fuel chamber.

CONTROLLING THE HEAT

If you need more heat, you can simply open the damper. If you need less heat, close it a little (or a lot).

If the wind is blowing in an unfavorable direction, instead of using the damper, you can consider pulling out the ash pan a little bit, or opening up the fuel door to get more air flowing.

SAFETY

The rocket stove gets very, very hot. Make sure to be extremely careful when you're near the rocket stove, and make sure to keep an eye on the kids at all times.

PUTTING THE FIRE OUT

Generally speaking, you'll want to just let the fire burn out. But if it's an emergency and you need to put the fire out right away, you can smother the fire with sand.

MAINTAINING YOUR STOVE

Maintenance is pretty easy. Just make sure you empty the ash pan regularly. And after every few uses, wipe down the stove with oil to prevent rust.

We've found that rocket stoves don't play nice with paint. Even high temperature paint doesn't stay on the rocket stove because the heat causes the stove itself to expand and contract, which cracks the paint. That lets moisture in, and leads to rust. So in our opinion, a plain old steel rocket stove is the way to go.

SKIPPY'S FAVORITE RECIPES

This isn't your average recipe book. For starters, we're cooking on rocket stoves. That means there won't be too much mention of exact temperature here or precise cooking times in many cases.

We give you cooking time estimates, but remember that everything depends on your own fuel, stove, food, cooking equipment, and even the weather. So as always, use your judgment.

But don't worry! We have full instructional videos so you can follow along if you get stuck. Just scan the QR code on each recipe (or tap it if you're reading the ebook version.)

And a quick note on serving sizes– if we don't give you a recommended amount of something, then that means you can cook as much (or little) of that ingredient as you like.

Our rules of thumb for success:

- Leave the damper open all the way most of the time; we'll tell you if you need to lower the heat
- Watch the food to make sure it doesn't burn
- Don't burn yourself!

Listen, these are Skippy's favorite meals. If he can whip them up, I promise you can, too.

And as mentioned earlier, you head over to **chiassonsmoke.com/rocket-stove-book** for a full list of resources, recommended food products, and more.

Oh and one more thing. If Skippy ever suggests he has a "faster" way of lighting the rocket stove... Do NOT take him up on the offer. Just trust me.

Now let's get cookin'!

PORK CHOPS WITH MUSHROOM CREAM SAUCE

INGREDIENTS

- Pork chops (as many as you'd like)
- Onions
- Minced garlic
- Chicken stock
- Mushrooms
- Heavy cream
- Flour

RECOMMENDED TOOLS

- Cast-iron skillet (or pan)
- Meat thermometer (optional)

Total cook time	Servings	Rocket Stove Attachment
30-45 minutes	3-6	Cross Top

INSTRUCTIONS

PREPARATION

Dice some onions and set them aside.

THE PORK

Fire up your rocket stove, place your pork chops on the pan, and get both sides nice and brown. Once they reach an internal temperature of around 145° F, you can take them off the grill and set them aside.

Now put your onions into the pan with the pork grease. Add a bit of chicken stock. When the onions are soft and brown, add a few spoonfuls of garlic. Let it cook a little bit, and stir it around so you don't burn the garlic. Then toss in mushrooms; use some pre-sliced ones if you want to save time. Let those cook just a bit, then add a whole stick of butter and let it melt down.

Thicken It Up

Now, mix in some flour. The amount is up to you, but we like to add enough for it to have a medium level of thickness. Add in some chicken stock to coat the bottom of the pan, and close the damper about halfway to reduce the heat.

Let that simmer for a while, and add in some heavy cream. You'll want to add enough to make the whole concoction the color of... Well... Cream.

Now put the fire out by closing the damper, and put the pork chops into the cream sauce. Don't forget to pour in the meat juice from the plate your pork was on, too.

At this point, you can close your damper all the way to reduce the heat even further.

Let it all simmer for another 10 minutes or so... And then that's it! You're done.

Sides

This goes great with mashed potatoes, which you can easily boil beforehand (on a separate stove) and mash while the chops are simmering in the final step.

FISH FRY

INGREDIENTS

- Fish filets (as many as you'd like)
- Peanut oil
- Eggs
- Hot sauce (we used Camp Dog)
- Mustard
- Flour
- Breading mix (We used Louisiana Seasoned Fish Fry breading mix)

RECOMMENDED TOOLS

- Tongs
- Spider skimmer
- Large bowl, or Tupperware container with lid
- Cast-iron skillet (or pan)

Total cook time	Servings	Rocket Stove Attachment
20-30 minutes	3-8	Cross Top

INSTRUCTIONS

PREPARATION

Get that rocket stove lit and pour peanut oil inside the pan. You'll want to add enough so the fish filets are completely covered when you add those in next.

COAT THE FILETS

Put some hot sauce in a bowl, add some mustard, and mix it together. (We like the Camp Dog Cajun Cayenne Pepper Hot Sauce.) Then use a brush to put a light coat of this mixture on the filets.

Then put some flour in a bowl and throw the filets in so they get covered. If you want to make it really easy, put the flour in a Tupperware container, put the lid on nice and tight, and shake it up.

Once the filets are coated with flour, place them aside. Then empty the bowl or container, or use a separate one, and put in some Louisiana Seasoned Fish Fry breading mix. We're gonna coat the filets one more time with this in a minute.

Scramble two eggs in a bowl. Then dip the filets into the egg wash, place them into the bowl or container again, and get them coated with the breading mix.

Fry 'Em Up

Then use tongs to add the filets into the oil. You should hear a nice crackling sound right as the filets go into the oil.

Let them fry until they're golden brown– it shouldn't take long, especially if you're using thin filets. Probably no longer than 3-5 minutes.

Grab them out with your spider skimmer (or tongs), place them on a plate or in a bowl with napkins, and let them cool down. You're all set!

LOUISIANA PORK, SAUSAGE, AND GRAVY

INGREDIENTS

- Rice (Optional)
- Pork chops (4-5)
- Onions (2)
- Bell paper (1)
- Celery (2 stalks)
- Smoked sausage (2)
- Water
- Cajun seasoning (we used Camp Dog)

RECOMMENDED TOOLS

- Cast iron Dutch oven (or pot) with lid
- Wooden spoon
- Large bowl

Total cook time	Servings	Rocket Stove Attachment
45 minutes	4-5	Cross Top

INSTRUCTIONS

PREPARATION

Dice up your onions, bell peppers, and celery, and mix them together. Chop up your sausage, too. Season your pork chops with whatever you like. We like using Camp Dog seasoning.

FRY UP THE PORK

Get your stove lit and toss your pork chop in the cast iron Dutch oven. Let it sear until it's brown and starts sticking to the bottom. Pour in a little water to prevent it from burning. Once it starts sticking again, pour a little more water in. Repeat this cycle at least three times.

On the fourth time, you can add onions, bell peppers, and celery. As they release water, use your wooden spoon to scrape the bottom to keep it from sticking.

You can throw in the sausage now too, and keep stirring to prevent sticking. Let the sausage turn brown in the process. Stir until all the moisture from the vegetables evaporates, then add water one last time to prevent it from burning.

Time for the Gravy

Now take a bowl of water and pour enough into the pot to cover all the meat. If your damper isn't all the way open, make sure it's open now so you can bring the water to a boil.

At this point, you can pour in more seasoning if you want.

Stir the mixture occasionally and scrape the sides and bottom of the pan to ensure you're not missing any flavor.

Lower the heat a bit by closing the damper about halfway, then let it simmer for around 30 minutes. Once the meat starts falling off the bones, it's ready to serve.

Try it with Rice

If you want to eat this with rice, now's the time to start preparing rice on another stove. Enjoy!

PORK JAMBALAYA

INGREDIENTS

- Pork butt (4lbs.)
- Smoked sausage (1lb.)
- Andouille sausage (1lb.)
- Cajun seasoning (we used Camp Dog)
- Oil
- Onions (4 cups)
- Bell peppers (2)
- Celery (1 cup)
- Minced garlic
- White rice (8 cups)
- Beef broth (8 cups)
- Parsely
- Green onion tops

RECOMMENDED TOOLS

- Cast iron Dutch oven (or large pot)
- Wooden spoon

Total cook time	Servings	Rocket Stove Attachment
45-60 minutes	8-10	Cross Top

INSTRUCTIONS

PREPARATION

Season your pork with cajun seasoning. Slice up your sausages nice and thin. Dice your onions, bell peppers, and celery, and mix it all together along with a bit of minced garlic.

The Pork

Once the rocket stove is nice and hot, add some oil so it coats the bottom. Then toss in the 4lbs. of pork butt and stir it around until it gets nice and brown. Then go ahead and toss in the 2lbs. of sausage.

The Veggies

When the sausage is brown on the edges, you can toss in the onions, bell peppers, celery, and minced garlic. Mix it together well.

Let it cook while stirring, until the vegetables are tender. Then mix in the 8 cups of rice and 8 cups of beef broth, along with 4 cups of water.

Wait for it to come to a boil, then close the rocket stove's damper all the way and put the lid on the pot.

Finishing Up

Let it cook until the rice is soft, then mix in some parsley and a small bowl of onion tops, mix it all around for a minute or two, then you're all set!

SHRIMP
AND GRITS

INGREDIENTS

- Bacon
- Shrimp
- Butter (1/4 stick)
- Onion (1)
- Bell pepper (1)
- Smoked andouille sausage
- Heavy cream
- Cajun seasoning (we used Cooking With Cajun's Spicy Voodoo Seasoning)
- Slap Ya Mama cajun seasoning (optional)
- Chicken stock
- Cheese

RECOMMENDED TOOLS

- Cast iron skillet (or pan)
- Tongs
- Paper towel
- Heat resistant gloves
- Small pot

Total cook time	Servings	Rocket Stove Attachment
30-45 minutes	4-6	Cross Top

INSTRUCTIONS

PREPARATION

Dice up your onion and bell pepper, and chop up your sausage.

THE BACON

Place the bacon in a smoking hot cast-iron skillet and sear until it reaches maximum crispiness for the best flavor.

Transfer the cooked bacon to a plate or tray with a paper towel on it, and set it aside.

The Veggies and Sausage

Throw in a quarter stick of butter to the same skillet and sauté the onions, bell peppers, and smoked andouille sausage until the vegetables are tender and the sausage is brown.

Pour in heavy cream, close your damper about halfway, and bring it to a simmer.

Add Spicy Voodoo seasoning to taste– adjust the amount based on your spice tolerance.

Once the sauce turns golden brown, remove the skillet from the heat.

The Shrimp

Get another pan ready to heat while you season the shrimp with Slap Ya Mama seasoning or your preferred cajun seasoning. You can keep the damper halfway closed. Cook the seasoned shrimp for 3-5 minutes. Remove the cooked shrimp from the pan, and place them on a plate or tray.

Remove the pan you used for the shrimp, and place the original pan (with the sauce) on the rocket stove. Now add the cooked shrimp into the sauce.

Pour a little chicken stock and let it simmer until it reaches your desired consistency. For our preference, we don't need much- just enough stock to loosen things up.

Once it's done, go ahead and take it off the stove and set it aside.

The Grits

Take your small pot and cook the grits as you like. I prefer to add some butter, cheese, and a little Slap Ya Mama seasoning.
The type of grits you decide to make will obviously affect the total cook time, so keep that in mind.

Serving

Pour the sauce onto the plate. Then, add a spoonful of grits, followed by some shrimp, the bacon you cooked earlier, and a sprinkle of onion on top.

You're done!

FRIED
MOREL MUSHROOMS

Fried mushrooms are more of a snack... But that doesn't stop Skippy from eating them like a full meal.

INGREDIENTS

- Morel mushrooms (as many as you like)
- Butter (1 stick)
- Flour
- Eggs
- Salt
- Pepper
- Garlic powder

RECOMMENDED TOOLS

- Cast iron skillet or pan
- Tongs
- Plate
- Paper towel

Total cook time	**Servings**	**Rocket Stove Attachment**
20 minutes	As many as you can get!	Cross Top

INSTRUCTIONS

PREPARATION

Cut the mushrooms in half, and soak them in water to clean them up.

Crack a few eggs into a bowl, and beat them until they're fully mixed. Set the bowl aside.

In a separate bowl, mix your flour with salt, pepper, and garlic powder. Set the bowl aside. Throw the butter into the pan, and close the damper about halfway so the pan reaches medium heat. (You don't want to burn your butter!) Let the butter melt down.

Fry 'Em Up

Put each of the mushrooms into the egg wash, then dip them in the flour mixture to coat them completely. Then throw each of them into the pan with melted butter.

Fry them until they're golden brown and slightly crispy around the edges.

Now, they're ready to serve! (And if you're like Skippy, you might wanna add a little bit more seasoning before serving.)

CAJUN CATFISH SAUCE PIQUANT

INGREDIENTS

- Catfish filet (3 lbs)
- Rice (optional)
- Corn (optional)
- Vegetable oil (1 cup)
- Flour (1 cup)
- Onion (1)
- Red bell pepper (1)
- Green bell pepper (1)
- Celery (2 stalks)
- Garlic (2 tablespoon)
- V8 Spicy Hot tomato juice
- Rotel (1 can)
- Tomato sauce (8 ounces)
- Tomato paste (3 ounces)
- Cajun seasoning (we used Camp Dog)

RECOMMENDED TOOLS

- Cast iron Dutch oven (or large pot)
- Wooden spoon
- Little jar
- Mixing bowl
- Plate

Total cook time	**Servings**	**Rocket Stove Attachment**
90 minutes	6-8	Cross Top

INSTRUCTIONS

PREPARATION

Dice up your bell peppers, celery, and garlic, and mix them together in a bowl.

Get your rocket stove started and close the damper about halfway so it reaches a medium heat. Then place your pot on the stove and pour in the vegetable oil.

The Hard Part

Add one-third of the flour and start stirring. Gradually add more flour, stirring each time until it's well mixed. Add the remaining flour and mix thoroughly until it reaches a nice caramel color. This is the most time-consuming part of the process, so do your best!

The Veggies

Throw in the vegetables and stir them for around 4-5 minutes until the vegetables are starting to get a bit softer.

Add a little tomato juice (maybe ⅓ of a soda-sized can of V8), stir it, and let it simmer in the pan for 4-5 minutes.

After the vegetables are nice and soft, add the 8 ounces of tomato sauce, the can of Rotel, and the 3 ounces of tomato paste. Mix it for 7-8 minutes until it reaches a thick consistency.

Add enough water to just cover the mixture, and add your preferred Cajun seasoning.

Open the damper all the way and wait until the mixture comes to a boil.

Once it starts boiling, reduce the heat by closing the damper about 80% of the way, and let the mixture simmer for around 20-30 minutes.

The Catfish

Lay your catfish filets in the sauce and let them simmer for another 20-30 minutes.

Sides

If you want rice or corn, now's the time to get that going on a separate stove. This meal also goes great with potato salad or fried shrimp.

Serving

After simmering, you're ready to serve. Get your rice and corn on a plate, and put some of your catfish and sauce right on top of the rice.

Enjoy!

HAMBURGER STEAK AND GRAVY

INGREDIENTS

- Ground meat (4 lbs)
- Egg (1)
- Cajun seasoning (we're using Camp Dog)
- Yellow onion (1)
- All-purpose flour
- Worcestershire sauce

RECOMMENDED TOOLS

- Cast iron skillet (or pan)
- Mixing bowl
- Gloves
- Plate
- Wooden spoon

Total cook time	Servings	Rocket Stove Attachment
30-45 minutes	3-5	Cross Top

INSTRUCTIONS

Preparation

Slice your onions into rings and set them aside. Then take the ground meat in a mixing bowl, crack an egg and mix it in, then add your cajun seasoning. Mix this up well and form patties of your preferred size. Put the pan on the stove and wait until it heats up.

The Patties

Place your hamburger patties on the pan and cook them to medium or medium-well. After they're done, place them on a plate and set them aside, trying to keep as much grease as possible in the pan for later use as it adds flavor.

The Onions

Once the meat is removed, add the sliced onions and start stirring. Then, add a little water, and stir well to prevent burning. You want the onions to mix with the meat grease flavor.

The Gravy

After the onions have softened and the water has evaporated, add half a cup of flour and mix well, then add a little water and continue mixing.

Keep adding water little by little until it begins to brown. Ensure nothing sticks to the bottom; if it does, use water to scrape it.

Putting It All Together

Once the mixture is nice and brown, add 4 cups of water. Once it reaches your preferred consistency, add back the hamburger patties. Drizzle it with Worcestershire sauce, and add a little more seasoning. Wait another 10-15 minutes to finish the cooking process.

> **Note From Skippy:** *"Worcestershire sauce?" I think you meant to say "wash your sister sauce." No need to thank me.*

Serving

Serve it over rice or mashed potatoes.

BLUE CRABS

INGREDIENTS

- Seafood seasoning (we used Louisiana Seafood Boil)
- Potatoes (6)
- Lemons (3)
- Corn (4 ears)
- Crabs
- Shrimp (optional)

RECOMMENDED TOOLS

- Seafood boil pot with basket (7.5 gallon)
- Spider skimmer

Total cook time	Servings	Rocket Stove Attachment
60 minutes	5-8	Cross Top

INSTRUCTIONS

Preparation

Get your rocket stove heated up, fill up your seafood boil pot about halfway to the top with water and place it on the stove top.

Slice your potatoes and lemons in half. Cut your ears of corn into 3rds. Then place them into the basket.

The Seasoning

Once your water is boiling, pour half a bag of your seafood seasoning into the water. (Our bag was about 4.5 lbs, so we poured 2.25 lbs of seasoning into the water.) Then place your basket into the boiling water.

Let the vegetables boil for about 20 minutes, or when the potatoes are soft. Then dump the vegetables out of the basket into a large bowl or other container. Now add the rest of your seasoning (another 2.25 lbs) into the water.

The Crabs

Fill your basket with crabs, place the basket into the water, and put the lid on the boil pot.

Let the crabs boil for 6 minutes (or until you see steam coming out of the side). Then close your damper all the way to let the heat die down, and remove the boil pot from the stove and place it on a stable surface.

Let the crabs sit for 20 minutes in the pot, then they'll be ready to go.

Sides

You can serve them with the corn and potatoes, and optionally boil some shrimp to add as well.

CRAWFISH ETOUFFEE

INGREDIENTS

- Steaks
- Potatoes
- Crawfish tails (1 lb) (we used Deshotels)
- Butter (2 sticks)
- Slap Ya Mama seasoning
- Flour (1 tbsp)
- Onion (1)
- Bell pepper (1)
- Celery (1 stick)
- Garlic

RECOMMENDED TOOLS

- Tongs
- Aluminum foil
- Medium-sized pot
- Small bowl
- Medium-sized bowl
- Wooden spoon
- PAM cooking spray

Total cook time	**Servings**	**Rocket Stove Attachment**
45-60 minutes	4-6	Grill Top

INSTRUCTIONS

Preparation

Mix the flour with ½ cup of water in a small bowl and set it aside.

Dice your onion, ½ of a bell pepper, and ½ a stick of celery, and put them in a medium-sized bowl together. Add a little bit of minced garlic to your desired taste. Set it aside.

Season your steaks as you wish– salt and pepper is enough if you don't feel like getting fancy.

The Potatoes

Put salt, pepper, and butter on your potatoes, then wrap them in aluminum foil and place them on the grill.

Turn the potatoes every 5 minutes or so.

Once they've been cooking for about 20 minutes, then put your pot in the middle of the stove and keep your potatoes off to the sides.

The Veggies

Close your damper about 80% of the way to reduce the heat, then put a stick of butter in the pot and let it melt down.

Add in the bowl of vegetables, and cook them until they're soft. While cooking them, don't forget to rotate the potatoes every few minutes.

The Crawfish Tails

Once the vegetables are soft, add in your 1 lb of crawfish tails. Let the juice from the bag of crawfish tails drip into the mixture for extra flavor. Add the Slap Ya Mama seasoning here too– you can add as much or little as you like. Mix it together.

Note From Skippy: *Where's y'all get those crawfish tails? "Deez hotels?" That don't even make sense.*

Now, close your damper all the way to bring the heat down, put the lid on the pot, and let it simmer for about 10 minutes.

Add your flour mixture to the pot, mix it together, place the lid back on, and let it simmer for another 10 minutes.

Keep Those Potatoes Warm

When the potatoes are soft, you can take them off the grill and rest them on the "V" shape of the rocket stove where the fuel chamber connects to the chimney. This will keep them warm, but not too warm.

Note From Skippy: Don't put the potatoes INSIDE the fuel chamber. Unless you want Boss to yell at ya.

The Steaks

Once the etouffee has been simmering for 10 minutes, pull the pot off the grill. Clean the grill a bit and oil it with PAM cooking spray.

Now open the damper all the way to increase the heat, and place your steaks on the grill. If you like rare or medium-rare, you'll want to grill the steaks for 1-2 minutes each side. You can cook them a bit longer if you don't like your food to have flavor.

While the steaks are finishing up, you can remove the potatoes from the warming rack and unwrap the foil.

Serving

You can put a steak and potato on each plate. Cut the potato in half, and scoop out some of the etouffee and smother the potato and steak with it.

BURGERS
ON THE GRILL

INGREDIENTS

- Hamburger patties
- Hamburger buns
- Ranch seasoning (optional) (we used Hidden Valley)
- Cheese slices (optional)
- Bacon (optional)
- Onions (1)
- Cajun seasoning (we used Camp Dog)
- Any desired condiments (ketchup, mustard, mayo, etc.)

RECOMMENDED TOOLS

- Small cast-iron skillet or pan
- Heat-resistant gloves
- Spatula

Total cook time	Servings	Rocket Stove Attachment
30 minutes	As many as you can get!	Grill Top

INSTRUCTIONS

Preparation

Slice up an onion and put the slices in a small skillet. Set it aside.

Form burger patties, and season them with whatever you like. We prefer our go-to cajun seasoning, Camp Dog. We also love using ranch seasoning– so if you haven't tried that yet, give it a shot!

The Best Part

If you're making bacon, you can throw that on the grill first and cook it to your desired crispiness.

After the bacon is done, you can close the damper 80% of the way to reduce the heat.

The Onions and Burgers

Clean off the grill gently, throw some onions in a small skillet and put that on the grill top. (You don't technically need the skillet, but if you're using the grill top, it prevents the onions from falling through the grill.) You can place the burger patties on the grill at the same time.

After a few minutes, the onions will be nice and soft. You can put on your heat-resistant gloves and take the skillet off the grill.

Flip the burgers for a few minutes, and don't forget to flip them when they're turning brown. You can also add more seasoning to them while they're on the grill.

The Wisconsin Element

Once the burgers are just about done, put a cheese slice on each patty, let it melt, then take the burgers off the grill with a spatula and place them on a plate.

The Rest

While the grill is still hot, you can optionally grill the burger buns for a minute or two. Now you have bacon, fried onions, and any condiments you like. Dress those burgers up however you see fit, and enjoy!

FAJITAS

INGREDIENTS

- Skirt steak
- Steak marinade
- Shrimp
- Green bell pepper (1)
- Red bell pepper (1)
- Yellow bell pepper (1)
- Onion (1)
- Shredded cheese
- Sour cream
- Tortillas
- Shrimp (optional)
- Chicken (optional)

RECOMMENDED TOOLS

- Cast-iron skillet (or pan)
- Heat-resistant gloves

Total cook time	Servings	Rocket Stove Attachment
30-40 minutes	Flexible	Cross Top

INSTRUCTIONS

Preparation

First, you'll want to find a good marinade. You can buy pre-made marinade packets at the grocery store, or you can whip up your own if you're feeling adventurous.

Put your skirt steak in a plastic storage bag along with the marinade, and let it marinate overnight in the refrigerator. If you're a little on the lazier side like our friend Skippy, you can get by with letting it soak for just 1 hour.

> **Note From Skippy:** *Some people call it lazy, but boss, I call it workin' "smarter" rather than "harter"... Whatever that means.*

If you want chicken in your fajitas, you can marinate it the same way in a different bag.

Now slice up your bell peppers and onion, and put them aside.

The Meat and Veggies

Fire up your rocket stove and place the skillet on it with the steak inside. Cook the steak about halfway, then add your vegetables.

If you want to add chicken, wait until the vegetables are starting to get a little soft (but still crunchy), then throw your chicken into the mix.

Let it cook until your vegetables are soft, then you can bring down the heat by closing the damper 80% of the way. If you want to add shrimp, now's the time to add those in and let them cook for a few minutes.

Once all the meat is ready to go, you can remove the skillet using your heat-resistant gloves.

The Tortillas

If you want to warm up your tortillas, you can place a new skillet or pan on the stove and let them get nice and warm (or crispy if that's your preference).

Serving

After that, you can throw the meat, shredded cheese, sour cream, and just about anything else on each tortilla and serve.

MACARONI AND CHEESE WITH HOTDOGS

If you've been counting, you know this is actually recipe #13, when we only promised 12.

Well, since this recipe is gourmet, we know it's not going to be possible for everyone to cook correctly. So we included it as a bonus for the culinary artists among our readers.

INGREDIENTS

- Macaroni
- Cheese powder
- Butter (1 stick)
- Milk
- Hot dog buns (optional)
- Hot dogs or sausages

RECOMMENDED TOOLS

- Medium-sized pot
- Strainer
- Grill
- Tongs
- Stainless steel spoon

Total cook time	Servings	Rocket Stove Attachment
15 minutes	Flexible	Grill Top (or cross top with an additional pan)

INSTRUCTIONS

Preparation

This recipe requires expert level attention and presence. So we recommend meditating for 20 minutes to get in the right headspace.

The Macaroni

Pour fresh water into your pot and wait until it boils. Then, add the macaroni to the boiling water.

After about 7 minutes, pour the macaroni into a strainer to drain the water.

Add room-temperature butter to your pot, and after it melts, pour the macaroni back in.

Add the cheese powder, then stir until well mixed.

Add a little milk and sauté it briefly, then your macaroni and cheese will be ready.

The Hotdogs

Get your grill ready and hot. Put the hot dogs on the grill and cook them to your preference.

Serving

At this point, you can choose to chop up the hot dogs and stir them into the macaroni, or place them on your hot dog buns and eat them separately.

And that's it!

DON'T
STOP THERE!

Well, you've reached the end of the book. But don't worry, that's not the end of the adventure. There's a lot more stuff you can whip up on the rockets!

We didn't want to leave you high and dry, so here are a few more ideas for meals that are especially suited to cooking on a rocket stove.

- Pancakes
- Omelettes
- Corned beef hash
- Chili
- Sloppy Joe
- Shrimp fried rice
- Fried shrimp po' boy
- Grilled cheese sandwiches
- Pizza
- Beer brats
- Pasta
- Loaded potatoes
- Lentil soup
- Vegetable stir fry
- Chicken alfredo

And hey, when you do some cooking on a rocket stove, don't forget to make a video and send it over! We always love seeing what others in the community are up to.

MORE
FROM US

Don't be a stranger! We love hearing what you have to say.

Give us a follow on your favorite social media platforms, and drop a comment letting us know what you thought of the book. (You might even find a video of Skippy's latest shenanigans.)

You can find us on social media here:

@chiassonsmoke

As a reminder, you can find all the resources mentioned in this book at the following URL:

https://chiassonsmoke.com/rocket-stove-book

And as always, don't forget to visit our main website:

https://chiassonsmoke.com

There, you can find high quality rocket stoves hand-made in Wisconsin, DIY weld kits, grills, fire pits, and a heck of a lot more.

Thanks for keeping our fire going by giving this book a read!

- Jason and Miranda

Made in United States
Orlando, FL
08 November 2024

53486445R00031